FREEDOM'S PROMISE

THE BIRTH OF
HIP-HOP

BY DUCHESS HARRIS, JD, PHD

WITH TAMMY GAGNE

Core Library

An Imprint of Abdo Publishing
abdobooks.com

Cover image: Run DMC became a popular hip-hop
group in the 1980s.

abdocorelibrary.com

Published by Abdo Publishing, a division of ABDO, PO Box 398166,
Minneapolis, Minnesota 55439. Copyright © 2020 by Abdo Consulting
Group, Inc. International copyrights reserved in all countries. No part of this
book may be reproduced in any form without written permission from the
publisher. Core Library™ is a trademark and logo of Abdo Publishing.

Printed in the United States of America, North Mankato, Minnesota
032019
092019

**THIS BOOK CONTAINS
RECYCLED MATERIALS**

Cover Photo: Waring Abbott/Michael Ochs Archives/Getty Images
Interior Photos: Waring Abbott/Michael Ochs Archives/Getty Images, 1; Raymond Boyd/Michael
Ochs Archives/Getty Images, 5; Pymcauig Universal Images Group/Newscom, 6–7; Leo Vals/
Hulton Archive/Getty Images, 10; Michael Ochs Archives/Getty Images, 12, 17, 43; Anthony
Barboza/Archive Photos/Getty Images, 14–15; Janette Beckman/Getty Images, 19; Doug Kanter/
AP Images, 22–23; Electric Pictures/Album/Newscom, 25; Red Line Editorial, 26, 36; Kevin Estrada/
MediaPunch/IPX/AP Images, 29; Mark Lennihan/AP Images, 32–33; Hayley Madden/Redferns/Getty
Images, 35; Jeff McCoy/Shutterstock Images, 38–39; Matt Sayles/Invision/AP Images, 40

Editor: Maddie Spalding
Series Designer: Claire Vanden Branden

Library of Congress Control Number: 2018966047

Publisher's Cataloging-in-Publication Data

Names: Harris, Duchess, author | Gagne, Tammy, author.
Title: The birth of hip-hop / by Duchess Harris and Tammy Gagne
Description: Minneapolis, Minnesota: Abdo Publishing, 2020 | Series: Freedom's promise |
    Includes online resources and index.
Identifiers: ISBN 9781532118692 (lib. bdg.) | ISBN 9781532172878 (ebook)
Subjects: LCSH: Hip-hop--Juvenile literature. | Hip-hop culture--Juvenile literature. | Rap
    (Music)--United States--Juvenile literature. | Rap (Music)--Social aspects--Juvenile
    literature.
Classification: DDC 781.649--dc23

CONTENTS

A LETTER FROM DUCHESS

When I was ten years old, I saved enough money to buy my first album. It was a hip-hop album by the Sugarhill Gang called *Rapper's Delight*. At such a young age, I did not have the language to express why I liked it so much, but I enjoyed the fact that my parents did not think it was "real" music. This is a common occurrence in American culture. Young people often create music that breaks away from the traditions of the previous generation. Hip-hop music is very different from other musical styles.

The hip-hop movement began in the 1970s. It included music and other forms of self-expression. Hip-hop music has evolved since then. The hip-hop music that my children listen to is different from *Rapper's Delight*. But it has similar themes and messages. It is still a way for Black people and minorities to express themselves. It continues to bring attention to social issues, such as discrimination and poverty. It has the power to inspire change. Please join me in exploring the history and evolution of hip-hop.

Duchess Harris

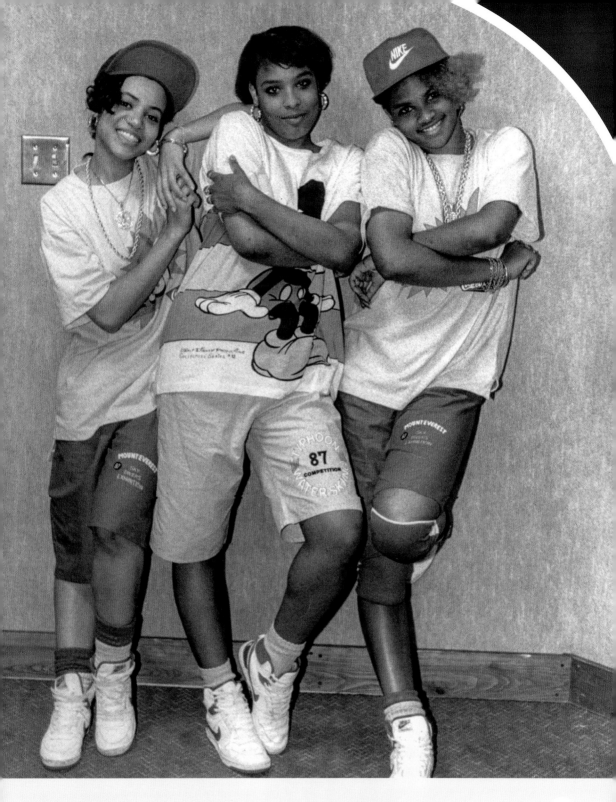

Salt-N-Pepa was one of the first all-female hip-hop groups.

CHAPTER
ONE

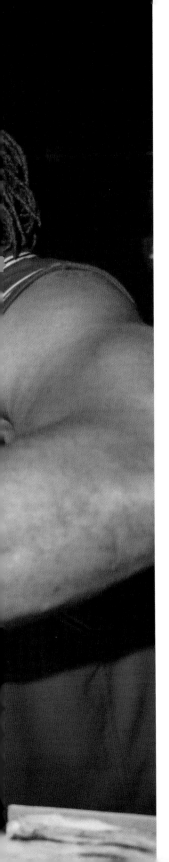

IT STARTED WITH A PARTY

I n 1973 Cindy Campbell wanted to buy some new clothes. It was almost time to head back to school in New York City. She did not want to show up in the same outfits that all her friends would be wearing. She wanted to shop at fancy clothing stores. But the clothes these stores sold were expensive. With her birthday coming up, Cindy got an idea. She would throw a huge party. She designed a flyer to invite many people. She charged them admission to get into her party.

Cindy knew her party had to be great to attract many people. Cindy asked her older brother, Clive, to be the disc jockey (DJ).

Clive Campbell, also known as DJ Kool Herc, looks through his records as he DJs at a party in England.

A DJ plays recorded music to entertain people. Clive was 16 years old. He had been born in Jamaica. He was influenced by Jamaican DJs. DJs in Jamaica were called selectors. Like these selectors, Clive spoke over his records as he spun them. The sound was unlike anything in the United States at this time.

MAKING DANCE MUSIC

When Clive Campbell began to DJ, he watched the people at the parties. He noticed that many of them would wait for a certain part of a song. When it played, they would dance or perform a special move. Most often the parts that people waited for were the drum breaks. This gave Clive an idea. He decided to play two copies of a record at once. He switched back and forth between them to make the drum breaks last longer.

Cindy's party took place on August 11, 1973. It was held in the Campbell family's apartment building in the Bronx. The Bronx is a neighborhood in New York City. The party was a huge success. Approximately 300 people came. The next day, people all over the Bronx were talking about DJ Kool Herc.

This was Clive's stage name. Herc stood for Hercules. His friends called him this because he was big and strong like the character Hercules. Today Clive is best known as the founder of hip-hop.

WHAT IS HIP-HOP?

Other DJs soon began copying DJ Kool Herc's style. They spun and scratched records. They spoke over the music with rhythm and flow. But hip-hop began to grow into more than just DJing. Many hip-hop artists also performed as masters of ceremonies (MCs). MCs were poets who recited their own

PERSPECTIVES

THE MEANING OF HIP-HOP

Afrika Bambaataa was the first person to use the term hip-hop publicly. Bambaataa is a DJ. He was also the leader of the Universal Zulu Nation. This group promotes hip-hop music and culture. Bambaataa linked the word *hip* to the feeling that hip-hop music inspired. *Hop* referred to the physical movement. Bambaataa recalled how he had first explained the term: "I said, 'This is hip and when you feel that music you gotta hop to it, so that's when we called it hip-hop.'"

verses to a beat. The result was the basis for today's rap music.

Hip-hop was not just music. It also included graphic art. Street artists painted colorful murals on public property, such as subway cars. Some artists made their names part of the artwork. This hip-hop graffiti style became known as tagging. Other artists danced in an acrobatic style called B-boying. This included impressive head and back spins. It would later become known as break dancing. Many break dancers performed in the streets.

All of these elements became part of hip-hop. But hip-hop was more than these things. It became a cultural movement. Music, art, and dance were all part of this movement. Hip-hop became a way for many young African Americans to express themselves.

At first hip-hop was only popular in New York City's African American communities, where it had started.

Graffiti tags were a common sight in 1970s New York City.

The Sugarhill Gang received a gold record for their song "Rapper's Delight" in 1980.

But interest soon spread beyond the city. In 1979 a black hip-hop group called the Sugarhill Gang recorded a song called "Rapper's Delight." They sampled music from the rhythm and blues (R&B) song "Good Times." Like MCs, they recited their own verses over the music. "Rapper's Delight" became widely popular. People around the country began to discover hip-hop.

STRAIGHT TO THE
SOURCE

The Paley Center for Media explains on its website how hip-hop is different from other music styles:

> *From the beginning, hip-hop was aggressive and oppositional, a break from the musical traditions it followed. . . . The music was not about the skillful arrangement of instruments but about the skillful production of sounds. When rap music included traditional melodies, they were more often compositions that others had made, "samples" from funk or R&B. . . . Most hip-hop music today is made up of more than the rapper and a DJ that made straight "rap" music back in the day—the most popular songs have a hook, a catchy chorus that breaks up the rapped verses. But then as now, hip-hop music is about the manipulation of sounds.*

> Source: "The Emergence of Hip-Hop." *The Paley Center for Media.* The Paley Center for Media, n.d. Web. Accessed January 18, 2019.

Consider Your Audience

Adapt this passage for a different audience, such as your friends. Write a blog post conveying this same information for the new audience. How does your post differ from the original text and why?

THE RISE OF HIP-HOP

As hip-hop music became popular, it also caused some controversy. Some people insisted that hip-hop music was not music. They said that the DJs were not composing original music but merely talking over other performers' works. The critics also did not like the sounds made by spinning and scratching the records. But many people did enjoy hip-hop. They saw it as a new form of musical expression. It did not follow traditional rules, and they liked that.

Many hip-hop music fans also embraced the murals that appeared in public places. They saw this artwork as a way for black

Grandmaster Flash and the Furious Five was one of the earliest hip-hop groups.

people to claim their place in society. It was a form of self-expression. Like the music, the tagging and graffiti often felt rebellious. But not everyone liked this artwork. Authorities removed the graffiti as quickly as possible. Law enforcement arrested people they caught tagging public property. Police worked hard to stop hip-hop artists before they could leave their marks.

While police tried to enforce graffiti laws, hip-hop art caught the attention of some well-known art dealers. Dealers as far away as Europe and Asia began to showcase hip-hop graffiti in art galleries. This encouraged society to view hip-hop graffiti as an art form.

FROM THE STREETS TO THE SCREENS

Break dancing was more widely popular than hip-hop music and graffiti. Many people were drawn to this new style of dance. Large crowds gathered in the streets to watch break dancers perform. People were impressed

Hip-hop graffiti and break dancing became popular in the 1970s and 1980s.

PERSPECTIVES

BREAK DANCING'S INFLUENCE

Break dancing was only popular for a short time. But it influenced many other styles of dance. In 2004 hip-hop dancer Beto Lopez explained how break dancing was still visible in popular culture. He said, "Each move now that Britney Spears or Justin Timberlake does takes a little bit of this and that from breakdancing . . . and blends it all in." Break dancing influenced a new style of hip-hop dance. This modern version focuses more on footwork than on gymnastics. Many of these moves are easy for hip-hop fans to learn.

by their moves. By the early 1980s, break dancing had been featured on television and in movies. Break dancers Wayne "Frosty Freeze" Frost and the Rock Steady Crew performed in the 1983 hit film *Flashdance*. The scene is still well known today. It created widespread interest in break dancing and hip-hop culture. One year later, R&B singer Chaka Khan featured break dancers Shabba Doo and Boogaloo

Richard "Crazy Legs" Colón was one of the leaders of the Rock Steady Crew.

Shrimp in the music video for her hit song "I Feel for You."

HIP-HOP FASHION

The hip-hop movement quickly became linked with a specific type of fashion. Fans loved the gold chains, jackets, hats, and sneakers that many hip-hop artists wore. Many fans began wearing similar clothing. Run DMC released a song in 1986 called "My Adidas." Adidas is a shoe and clothing company. The song was about Adidas-brand sneakers. After the song became popular, Adidas offered the hip-hop group an endorsement deal. The company paid Run DMC $1 million to appear in ads wearing Adidas sneakers.

Movies about hip-hop culture were wildly successful. This included the movies *Beat Street* and *Breakin'*. Break dancing was featured in these films. But the public's fascination with break dancing did not last as long as its attraction to other aspects of hip-hop. As the hip-hop movement grew, other parts of hip-hop culture became more popular.

Hip-hop was entirely different from other music styles. But hip-hop artists often borrowed from other types of music. Some musical groups even worked with hip-hop artists to create music that combined styles. In 1986 Run DMC recorded a cover of the song "Walk This Way." The rock band Aerosmith had made the song famous in 1975. The band appeared in Run DMC's video for the remake. The song's popularity made Run DMC the most famous hip-hop stars at that time. The song made it into the top-five list of songs on the pop music charts.

EXPLORE ONLINE

Chapter Two discusses how people reacted to hip-hop graffiti. The article below also explores this topic. How is the information from the article the same as the information in Chapter Two? What new information did you learn from the article?

HIP HOP, PUNK, AND THE RISE OF GRAFFITI IN 1980S NEW YORK
abdocorelibrary.com/hip-hop

CHAPTER THREE

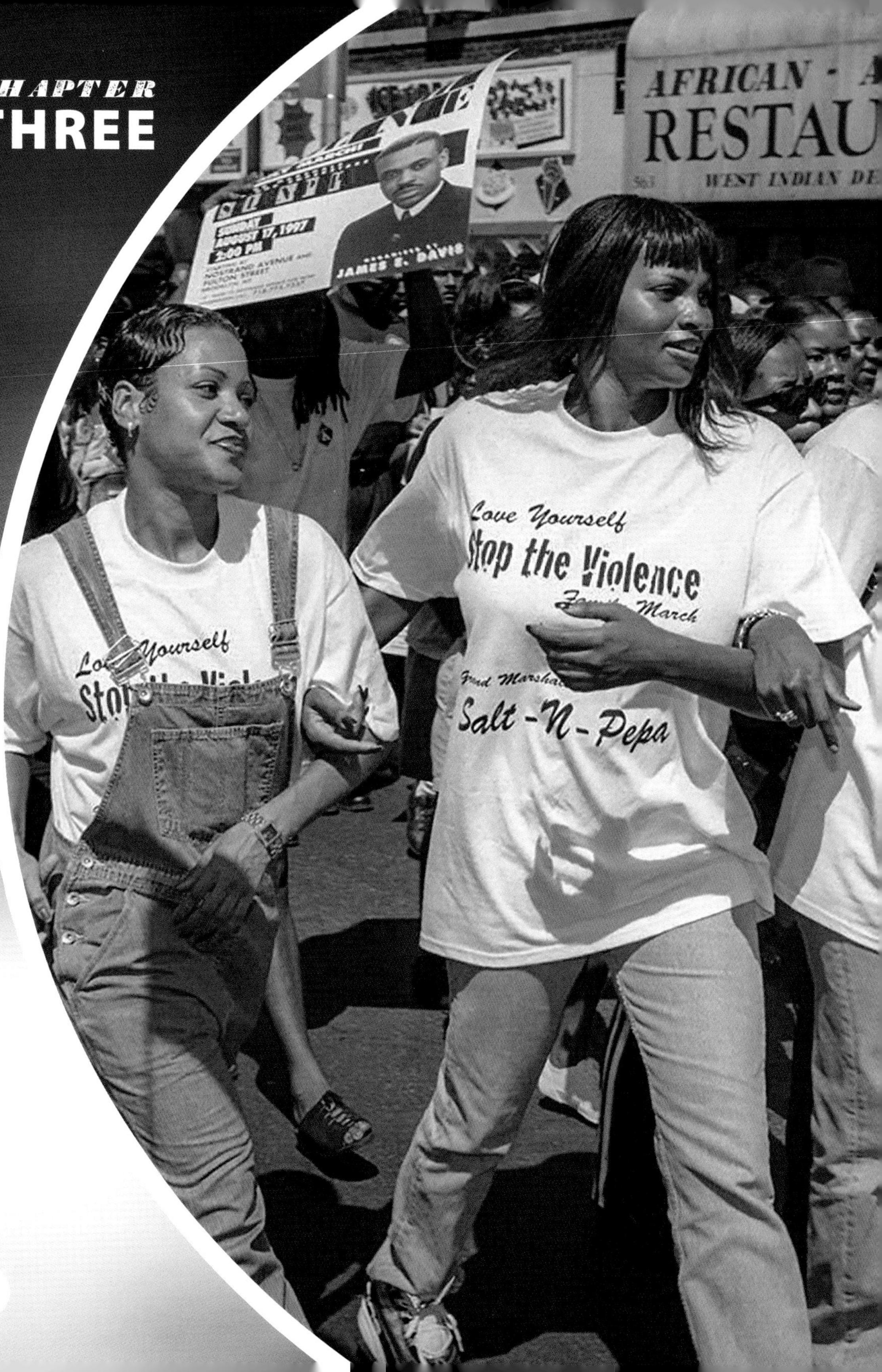

HIP-HOP'S MESSAGE

Despite hip-hop's rising popularity in the 1980s and 1990s, many people did not like it. One of the reasons people disliked hip-hop was because of its link to violence. Some people thought the movement encouraged dangerous behavior. Many artists mentioned violence in their songs. Some committed violent crimes. News stories about these events strengthened hip-hop's link to violence. Some people called the music "gangster rap." Many people associated black people with crime. This stereotype influenced their thoughts about black hip-hop artists.

Hip-hop group Salt-N-Pepa joined a march against violence in Brooklyn, New York, in 1997.

Public concern about hip-hop music increased when some hip-hop artists died in gang shootings or stabbings. Many black hip-hop artists lived in low-income neighborhoods. These areas had high rates of crime. One of the most notable artists to die from gang violence was Tupac Shakur. The African American rapper was killed in a drive-by shooting in Las Vegas, Nevada, in 1996. Another famous black rapper was killed in a similar way six months later. Christopher Wallace was shot in a drive-by shooting in Los Angeles, California. Wallace was better known by his stage names Biggie Smalls or the Notorious B.I.G.

Some hip-hop music also reflected black artists' dislike of the police. Police often discriminated against African Americans. They targeted and unjustly arrested black people. Rap songs made more people aware of how the police mistreated African Americans. Still, many people blamed rap music for the rise of violence.

Rapper Tupac
Shakur's murder is
still unsolved.

Some rappers wrote songs about killing cops who
committed police brutality. This made some listeners
uncomfortable. But that was the point. Artists wanted
listeners to understand how they felt. They used their
music to speak out about the injustices they saw in
their neighborhoods.

In 1991 four police officers beat a black man named
Rodney King in Los Angeles. The officers were tried
one year later. They were found not guilty of any crime.
Many people were outraged by this outcome. Riots
erupted in the city. Some hip-hop artists responded

CRIME AND HIP-HOP

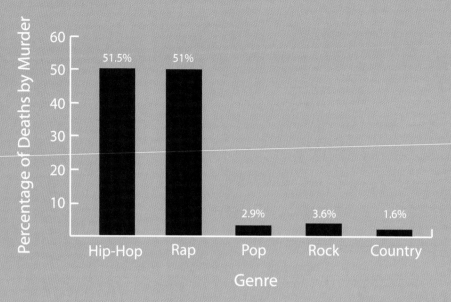

The above graph shows the percentage of deaths among hip-hop artists that were murders. It also shows the percentage of deaths among artists of other genres that were murders. Why do you think this number is higher for hip-hop artists and rappers than for artists of other genres?

with their music. The artists Ice Cube, Ice-T, and Dr. Dre wrote songs about the injustice.

Not all hip-hop music glorified violence. Some hip-hop songs discouraged violence. In 1988 a man was stabbed to death at a hip-hop concert in New York. Several MCs responded by recording a song called "Self Destruction." Hip-hop group Public Enemy and other artists helped create and perform the song. The song was the first effort of a new movement they began called Stop the Violence. Its purpose was to end violence in black communities.

Hip-hop artists shared their struggles in their music. In 1982 hip-hop group Grandmaster Flash and the Furious Five recorded a song called "The Message." It explored the long-term effects of growing up in a low-income neighborhood. It inspired many other

PERSPECTIVES
DISCOURAGING GUN VIOLENCE

Snoop Dogg is a popular rapper. In 2013 he recorded a song called "No Guns Allowed." The song is about school shootings. In it, Snoop Dogg raps, "Let the music play, me don't want no more gunplay. . . . Me don't want to see no more youth dead." Snoop Dogg recorded the song with his daughter. In an interview with *Rolling Stone* magazine, he explained the purpose of the song. He said, "We just want to prevent the next [school shooting] from happening. That's what it's all about, trying to bring awareness and push love and peace."

artists to make meaningful music. Many people consider "The Message" to be the most influential hip-hop song of all time.

WOMEN AND HIP-HOP

Some people also associated hip-hop with misogyny, or a hatred of women. Many rap songs spoke about women in disrespectful ways. Some songs called women terrible names or only spoke about them as sex objects. Critics of hip-hop worried about the effects of this part of the hip-hop movement. They were concerned that young fans would learn to mistreat women from listening to rap music. When rap songs played on the radio, the bad words were usually bleeped out. But many people believed that this just made listeners more interested in the parts that had been left out.

One of the most powerful weapons against hip-hop's misogyny was female rappers. Many of them used their own music to condemn the mistreatment of women. They also encouraged other women to demand

Throughout her career, Queen Latifah has pushed against the antifeminist messages common in hip-hop music.

better treatment. Queen Latifah's song "U.N.I.T.Y." was filled with positive messages for women. She made it clear that it was not okay for men to insult her or other women. The song was popular. It won the Grammy Award for Best Rap Solo Performance in 1995. Other well-known female rappers included Salt-N-Pepa, Missy Elliott, and Lauryn Hill. These artists also sang songs with empowering lyrics for women.

INSPIRING YOUNG ARTISTS

No one could deny that hip-hop had its share of problems. But it also brought many young people into the arts. Many kids were drawn to hip-hop music and culture. Kids do not need to come from wealthy families to become hip-hop artists. Rapping does not require any musical instruments. One of the most popular parts of hip-hop music is called beatboxing. Beatboxers make drum sounds with their voices. Beatboxing requires talent and practice but not money.

Many hip-hop artists are passionate about respect and social justice. These messages come through in their songs. Hip-hop artists often come from poor areas with high crime rates.

HIP-HOP AND RAP

Some people think hip-hop and rap music are the same thing. These music styles do share many qualities. But hip-hop is a culture. Like break dancing and graffiti, hip-hop music is just one part of hip-hop culture. Rap music is a style that came from hip-hop. It focuses more on rhyming and poetry than other types of hip-hop music.

In these areas, some people sell drugs or join gangs because they do not have many opportunities. Many hip-hop artists use their music to speak out about this problem. For example, rapper Jay-Z explores his childhood in poverty in his song "Izzo (H.O.V.A.)." Jay-Z also talks about his experiences with violence and crime in his songs. Rapper Lupe Fiasco explains how hip-hop inspired him to stay away from a life of crime in his song "Hip-Hop Saved My Life."

FURTHER EVIDENCE

Chapter Three explores how hip-hop culture evolved in the 1980s and 1990s. What was one of the main points of this chapter? What evidence is included to support this point? Read the article at the website below. Does the information on the website support the main point of the chapter? Does it present new evidence?

ABOUT HIP-HOP: TIMELINE
abdocorelibrary.com/hip-hop

CHAPTER
FOUR

HIP-HOP'S LEGACY

Hip-hop has come a long way over the years. For a long time, music awards shows such as the Grammy Awards did not acknowledge hip-hop. That changed in 1987. But hip-hop musicians did not receive their own category at this time. Instead they were put in the R&B category. This was another category of music that was dominated by black artists. Hip-hop artists had to compete with R&B musicians. Two years later, the Grammys finally added a hip-hop category. But it was awarded off the air. It seemed that hip-hop had taken one step forward followed by a big step back.

Run DMC arrives at the 1988 Grammy Awards.

Hip-hop artists Salt-N-Pepa, LL Cool J, and Kool Moe Dee boycotted the Grammys in 1989. They believed the awards show disrespected them and other hip-hop artists. Hip-hop duo DJ Jazzy Jeff & the Fresh Prince won the first Grammy for a rap song in 1989. But they had also boycotted the show. The Fresh Prince is now better known by his given name, Will Smith.

Rapper Lauryn Hill performs at a concert in the United Kingdom in 1999.

HIP-HOP AWARDS

1993
Arrested Development became the first rap act to win a Grammy for Best New Artist.

1998
Diddy became the first rapper to win more than one Grammy in one year.

1990
Young MC became the first solo rapper to win a Grammy.

1996
Naughty by Nature became the first group to win a Grammy for Best Rap Album.

2018
Rapper Jay-Z won the Salute to Industry Icons Award at the Grammys.

The above timeline shows some of the awards and recognitions hip-hop artists have received. How does this timeline reflect hip-hop's influence? Do you think more hip-hop artists will be recognized in the future? Why or why not?

Grammy awards in the hip-hop category are now usually presented on the air. Rappers often receive nominations in other categories too. They have been nominated for best album, best record, and best song of the year. MC Hammer was the first rapper nominated for Record of the Year for "U Can't Touch This" in 1991. Lauryn Hill was the first rapper to win a Grammy for Album of the Year in 1999. Hip-hop duo Outkast won this award in 2004. Still, hip-hop artists rarely win Grammys. Rappers often win for their performances in other people's songs. Many people think the awards show favors white artists over black artists. Most nominees and winners are white artists.

EFFECTS ON SOCIETY

Despite its struggles, hip-hop has had a largely positive influence on society. Hip-hop has given people of color and people who live in poor communities a voice. They can communicate their experiences and advocate for change through hip-hop music.

Hip-hop music and culture were once only popular within a few communities. Today hip-hop is popular around the world. Hip-hop is more

SEXISM IN HIP-HOP

The number of female hip-hop artists is growing. But sexism is still common in this genre. People often have certain expectations of female artists. They may be expected to look and act like male artists. Or they may be expected to look sexy. Some hip-hop artists, such as Nicki Minaj, are trying to combat these stereotypes. Minaj thinks that female artists should be taken just as seriously as male artists. She thinks there is still much progress to be made in this area.

Black Lives Matter activists protest police brutality.

than just a form of entertainment. Hip-hop music

educates people about important social issues, such

as poverty and gang violence. Many hip-hop artists

have also joined the Black Lives Matter movement. This movement brings attention to police violence against African Americans.

Popular rapper Kendrick Lamar supports the Black Lives Matter movement.

Hip-hop has become the most popular type of music in the United States. For years this honor belonged to rock music. But in 2017, rappers such as Drake and Kendrick Lamar made hip-hop the top-selling genre in the country. With an audience this large, there is no telling what this cultural movement will accomplish in the future.

STRAIGHT TO THE
SOURCE

Chuck D began his hip-hop career as a member of Public Enemy. In an interview with *Esquire* magazine, he shared some of the advice he gives young people:

> I tell songwriters I work with, "You're writing a song, but I'd also like to see if you can write a paragraph about that song, because if you can't have a discussion about your song, you're relying on luck." Sometimes luck makes a one-hit wonder, but if you want to become a skilled craftsman and you want to write songs that stand the test of time—that look at the environment and answer to it—you have to be able to express that. There are a lot of hip-hop and rap writers who are incredible but who have neglected that area, and other artists are not covering them because they're just not skilled at their art.

Source: Jeff Slate. "Chuck D. Is on a Mission to Protect the History of Hip-Hop." *Esquire Magazine*. Esquire Magazine, October 13, 2017. Web. Accessed November 30, 2018.

Back It Up

The author of this passage is using evidence to support a point. Write a paragraph describing the point the author is making. Then write down two or three pieces of evidence the author uses to make the point.

FAST FACTS

- The hip-hop movement began with a birthday party in the Bronx on August 11, 1973. DJ Kool Herc is known as the founder of hip-hip. His real name was Clive Campbell.

- Hip-hop was the basis for modern rap music. Hip-hop culture includes hip-hop music, graffiti art, and dancing. B-boying and break dancing are styles of hip-hop dance.

- Hip-hop music created controversy at first. Some people did not see the DJs or MCs as artists because they often borrowed from other musicians.

- Some people also disliked the graffiti that hip-hop artists painted on public property. But many others saw the graffiti as art. Hip-hop art and music were ways for people to express themselves.

- One of the reasons some people did not like hip-hop was because it was linked to violence and gangs. But many hip-hop artists discouraged violence.

- It took a long time for the music industry to recognize hip-hop as a real music style. Today it is the most popular type of music in the country.

STOP AND
THINK

Surprise Me

Chapter One explores how the hip-hop movement began.
After reading this book, what two or three facts about
the history of hip-hop did you find most surprising? Write
a few sentences about each fact. Why did you find each
fact surprising?

Take a Stand

Misogyny and violence are still present in some of today's
hip-hop songs. There is also still sexism in the hip-hop
industry. How do you think the hip-hop industry could
address these problems?

Why Do I Care?

Maybe you are not a fan of hip-hop music. But that doesn't
mean you can't think about its influence on society. What
lessons do you think can be found in hip-hop music? Do you
think anyone could learn something from listening to this
genre? Why or why not?

GLOSSARY

boycott
to stage a protest by refusing to buy a product or attend an event

cultural appropriation
the act of taking parts of another group's culture and using it for personal gain

endorsement
public approval, often done through advertising

genre
a category or style of music

glorify
to make something seem attractive or admirable

misogyny
dislike or prejudice against women

rhythm and blues (R&B)
a style of music similar to jazz that was made popular by African Americans in the 1940s

riot
violent and uncontrolled behavior by a group of people

sample
to use part of a recording from another performer

sexism
discrimination against women because of their sex

stereotype
a common belief about a group of people that is usually negative and untrue

ONLINE
RESOURCES

To learn more about the birth of hip-hop, visit our free resource websites below.

Visit **abdocorelibrary.com** or scan this QR code for free Common Core resources for teachers and students, including vetted activities, multimedia, and booklinks, for deeper subject comprehension.

Visit **abdobooklinks.com** or scan this QR code for free additional online weblinks for further learning. These links are routinely monitored and updated to provide the most current information available.

LEARN
MORE

Bailer, Darice. *African-American Culture*. Minneapolis: Abdo Publishing, 2014.

Kramer, Barbara. *Lin-Manuel Miranda: Award-Winning Musical Writer*. Minneapolis: Abdo Publishing, 2018.

ABOUT THE
AUTHORS

Duchess Harris, JD, PhD
Dr. Harris is a professor of
American Studies at Macalester
College and curator of the Duchess
Harris Collection of ABDO books.
She is also the coauthor of the titles in
the collection, which features popular
selections such as *Hidden Human
Computers: The Black Women of NASA*
and series including News Literacy and
Being Female in America.

Before working with ABDO, Dr. Harris authored several other books
on the topics of race, culture, and American history. She served as an
associate editor for *Litigation News*, the American Bar Association
Section of Litigation's quarterly flagship publication, and was the first
editor in chief of *Law Raza*, an interactive online journal covering race
and the law, published at William Mitchell College of Law. She has
earned a PhD in American Studies from the University of Minnesota and
a JD from William Mitchell College of Law.

Tammy Gagne

Tammy Gagne has written dozens of books for both adults and
children. Her other titles in this series include *Carol Moseley
Braun: Politician and Leader* and *Richard Wright: Author
and World Traveler*. She lives in northern New England
with her husband, son, and a menagerie of pets.

INDEX